STRESS

STRESS

Life Application® Bible Studies ™

Valerie Weidemann
James C. Galvin, Ed.D.

Tyndale House Publishers, Inc.
Wheaton, Illinois

Life Application Bible Studies: *Stress*. Copyright © 1996 by Tyndale House Publishers, Inc., Wheaton, Illinois 60189. All rights reserved.

Cover illustration copyright © 1996 by José Ortega. All rights reserved.

Developed exclusively for Tyndale House Publishers by The Livingstone Corporation. Bruce B. Barton, David R. Veerman, Daryl J. Lucas, Michael Kendrick, Christopher D. Hudson, James C. Galvin, Valerie Weidemann, project staff.

Life Application notes are adapted from the *Life Application Bible*, © 1988, 1989, 1990, 1991 by Tyndale House Publishers, Inc. All rights reserved.

Life Application is a registered trademark of Tyndale House Publishers, Inc.

Life Application Bible Studies is a trademark of Tyndale House Publishers, Inc.

Scripture quotations marked KJV are taken from the *Holy Bible,* King James Version.

Scripture quotations marked NIV are taken from the *Holy Bible,* New International Version®. NIV®. Copyright © 1973, 1978, 1984 by International Bible Society. Used by permission of Zondervan Publishing House. All rights reserved.

Scripture quotations marked NLT are taken from the *Holy Bible,* New Living Translation, copyright © 1996. Used by permission of Tyndale House Publishers, Inc., Wheaton, Illinois 60189. All rights reserved.

ISBN 0-8423-0165-8

Printed in the United States of America

00 99 98 97 96
8   7   6   5   4   3   2

Contents

A Note to Bible Study Leaders

Trying to use something that does not work often brings frustration and disappointment. On the other hand, using something that works well is a delight. The Life Application Bible Studies are the latter, especially if you want to help the people in your small group apply the Bible to their lives. That is because these are the most application-oriented Bible study guides available, covering a variety of topics to meet a range of interests and needs.

WHAT IS APPLICATION?

The best way to define application is to first determine what it is *not*. Application is *not* just accumulating knowledge. This helps us discover and understand facts and concepts, but it stops there. History is filled with philosophers who knew what the Bible said but failed to apply it to their lives, keeping them from believing and changing. Many think that understanding is the goal of Bible study, but it is really only the beginning.

Application is *not* illustration. Illustration only tells us how someone else handled a similar situation. While we may empathize with that person, we still have little direction for our personal situation.

Application is *not* just making a passage "relevant." Making the Bible relevant only helps us to see that the same lessons that were true in Bible times are true today; it does not show us how to apply them to the problems and pressures of our individual lives.

What, then, is application? Application begins by knowing and understanding God's Word and its timeless truths. *But we cannot stop there.* If we do, God's Word may not change our life, and studying the Bible may become dull, difficult, tedious, and tiring. A good application focuses on the truth of God's Word, shows the reader what to do about what is being read, and motivates the reader to respond to what God is teaching. All three are essential to application.

Application is putting into practice what we already know (see Mark 4:24 and Hebrews 5:14) and answering the question "So what?" by confronting us with the right questions and motivating us to take action (see 1 John 2:5-6 and James 2:26). Application is deeply personal—unique for each individual. It is making a relevant truth a personal truth and involves developing a strategy and action plan to live your life in harmony with the Bible. It is the biblical "how to" of life.

This is what the Life Application Bible Studies were designed to do—to make relevant truth personal and to help you live your life in harmony with the Bible.

ABOUT THIS STUDY GUIDE

Each Life Application Bible Study is made up of six lessons. The lessons are divided into four easy-to-lead sections. The first section, entitled "Starter," contains two interesting questions that will get your group talking. It also introduces your group to the area of life covered by the lesson.

The second section, entitled "Study," contains three sets of verses, notes, and questions. The verses appear in three different translations of the Bible— King James Version (KJV), New International Version (NIV), and the New Living Translation (NLT). You can select the translation you and your group prefer or read all three comparatively. The notes summarize the point of the passage quickly and help your group see how the passage applies to their lives. The questions help your group examine God's view on the topic as well as their own views. In addition, the questions help your group members think about practical steps they can take to apply God's Word to their lives.

The third section, entitled "Summary," reviews the important points in each lesson and calls the participants to action.

The fourth section, entitled "Supplemental Questions," gives you additional Bible passages, notes, and questions to extend the lesson or to replace some of the passages from the "Study" section.

USING THIS STUDY GUIDE

Begin each lesson with prayer, asking the Holy Spirit for guidance through and wisdom for your study. Then begin the study, working your way through the

Starter, Study, and Summary sections of the lesson. Here are the recommended time allotments for each section of a lesson based on a sixty- or ninety-minute study:

Section	60-Minute Study	90-Minute Study
Starter:	5 minutes	10 minutes
Study: first passage	15 minutes	20 minutes
Study: second passage	15 minutes	20 minutes
Study: third passage	15 minutes	20 minutes
Summary	10 minutes	20 minutes

The time allotments are only suggestions. Larger groups may require more time for discussion. Also, some groups may be more talkative than others, so the time required to complete the studies will vary from group to group. When you have finished the lesson, end your study with prayer.

ADAPTING THIS STUDY GUIDE

The Life Application Bible Studies have been designed for groups to work through in six weeks, but they can easily be adapted to extend the study to twelve weeks. Here are some alternatives for extending the study:

LENGTH	SECTIONS
12 weeks (slower)	Work through the Starter section and one or two passages from the Study section the first week. Then work through the last passage from the Study section and the Summary section for the next week.
12 weeks (deeper)	Work through the Starter and Study sections the first week. Then select three supplemental passages from the Supplemental Questions section and work through these passages as well as the Summary section for the next week.

THE GOAL OF THIS STUDY GUIDE

No note, by itself, can apply Scripture directly to your life. It can only teach, direct, inspire, recommend, and urge. It can give you the resources and direction you need to apply the Bible. But only *you* can take these resources and put them into practice. James said it clearly:

> *Do not merely listen to the word, and so deceive yourselves. Do what it says. Anyone who listens to the word but does not do what it says is like a man who looks at his face in a mirror and, after looking at himself, goes away and immediately forgets what he looks like. But the man who looks intently into the perfect law that gives freedom, and continues to do this, not forgetting what he has heard, but doing it—he will be blessed in what he does.*

James 1:22-25, NIV

LESSON ONE

No Pain, No Gain

••

Family conflict, disagreements with friends, pressure on the job, health problems, and overdue bills—stress fills every corner of life. Though we may be able to reduce the amount we are facing, we can never completely eliminate stress from our lives. But where can we find help for dealing with the stress we face? The most reliable source is God. The Bible uses such words as *trials, suffering, troubles, conflict,* and *pressure* to describe stress. This lesson will help you understand the biblical perspective on stress. You will learn that God uses stress to strengthen your character and to demonstrate his power by helping you handle the pressure.

◆◆◆◆ *STARTER*

1. *In what ways do people typically respond to stress?*

2. *What good results have you experienced from stress?*

◆◆◆◆◆◆◆ **STUDY**

Read the following three sets of Bible passages and application notes.
Answer the questions for each set before moving on to the next.

┌─ **Romans 5:3-5** ───

KJV	NIV	NLT
And not only so, but we glory in tribulations also: knowing that tribulation worketh patience; and patience, experience; and experience, hope: And hope maketh not ashamed; because the love of God is shed abroad in our hearts by the Holy Ghost which is given unto us.	Not only so, but we also rejoice in our sufferings, because we know that suffering produces perseverance; perseverance, character; and character, hope. And hope does not disappoint us, because God has poured out his love into our hearts by the Holy Spirit, whom he has given us.	We can rejoice, too, when we run into problems and trials, for we know that they are good for us—they help us learn to endure. And endurance develops strength of character in us, and character strengthens our confident expectation of salvation. And this expectation will not disappoint us. For we know how dearly God loves us, because he has given us the Holy Spirit to fill our hearts with his love.

Paul said that Christians can rejoice when experiencing difficulties. Believers can rejoice in suffering, not because they like pain or deny its tragedy, but because they know God is using life's difficulties to build their character. The problems they run into will develop their perseverance—which in turn will strengthen their character, deepen their trust in God, and give them greater confidence about the future. We can thank God for the strength he provides to handle the stress that comes each day.

3. *How can pressure and suffering produce positive rather than negative results?*

4. *How can hope affect someone's attitude toward stress?*

5. *What keeps Christians from rejoicing when they are experiencing stressful circumstances?*

6. *How can the stress you are currently facing help you develop patience and endurance?*

---

1 Peter 1:6-7

KJV	NIV	NLT
Wherein ye greatly rejoice, though now for a season, if need be, ye are in heaviness through manifold temptations: That the trial of your faith, being much more precious than of gold that perisheth, though it be tried with fire, might be found unto praise and honour and glory at the appearing of Jesus Christ.	In this you greatly rejoice, though now for a little while you may have had to suffer grief in all kinds of trials. These have come so that your faith—of greater worth than gold, which perishes even though refined by fire—may be proved genuine and may result in praise, glory and honor when Jesus Christ is revealed.	So be truly glad! There is wonderful joy ahead, even though it is necessary for you to endure many trials for a while. These trials are only to test your faith, to show that it is strong and pure. It is being tested as fire tests and purifies gold—and your faith is far more precious to God than mere gold. So if your faith remains strong after being tried by fiery trials, it will bring you much praise and glory and honor on the day when Jesus Christ is revealed to the whole world.

As gold is heated, impurities float to the top and can be skimmed off. Steel is tempered, or strengthened, by heating it in fire. Likewise, the stress that Christians experience from trials, struggles, and persecution refines and strengthens their faith, making them useful to God. Begin today to view the stress in your life as part of the refining process that is preparing you to meet Christ.

7. *How have your past trials strengthened and refined your faith?*

8. *How can a stressed-out Christian bring glory to God?*

9. *What are a few of the pressures that you are facing right now at home, school, work, or church?*

10. *What can you do now to strengthen your faith so that you will be better prepared to face stress in the future?*

Daniel 3:28-29

KJV

Then Nebuchadnezzar spake, and said, Blessed be the God of Shadrach, Meshach, and Abed-nego, who hath sent his angel, and delivered his servants that trusted in him, and have changed the king's word, and yielded their bodies, that they might not serve nor worship any god, except their own God. Therefore I make a decree, That every people, nation, and language, which speak any thing amiss against the God of Shadrach, Meshach, and Abed-nego, shall be cut in pieces, and their houses shall be made a dunghill: because there is no other God that can deliver after this sort.

NIV

Then Nebuchadnezzar said, "Praise be to the God of Shadrach, Meshach and Abednego, who has sent his angel and rescued his servants! They trusted in him and defied the king's command and were willing to give up their lives rather than serve or worship any god except their own God. Therefore I decree that the people of any nation or language who say anything against the God of Shadrach, Meshach and Abednego be cut into pieces and their houses be turned into piles of rubble, for no other god can save in this way."

NLT

Then Nebuchadnezzar said, "Praise to the God of Shadrach, Meshach, and Abednego! He sent his angel to rescue his servants who trusted in him. They defied the king's command and were willing to die rather than serve or worship any god except their own God. Therefore, I make this decree: If any people, whatever their race or nation or language, speak a word against the God of Shadrach, Meshach, and Abednego, they will be torn limb from limb, and their houses will be crushed into heaps of rubble. There is no other god who can rescue like this!"

King Nebuchadnezzar had commanded everyone to bow down and worship the image of gold that he had set up, with the warning that whoever refused would be thrown into a blazing furnace. Shadrach, Meshach, and Abednego chose to stay true to their beliefs, regardless of the consequences. As a result, the king acknowledged the power of the one true God. Remember that the way you choose to handle stress serves as a testimony to others. Rely on God to help you stand strong so that others will be convinced of God's power.

11. *Under what circumstances are believers most vulnerable to life's pressures?*

12. *How does the way you handle stress affect the people around you?*

13. *When have you been encouraged through the example of a Christian friend who handled stress well?*

14. *What changes could you make in the way you deal with stress so that others can see God working in you?*

◆◆◆◆◆◆◆ **SUMMARY**

No one likes to experience hardship and pain, but these three passages reveal that the stress God allows in life can be good for Christians and helpful to others. If Christians depend on Christ's power during difficult times, their character will be strengthened. In fact, the faith of Christians is often proven genuine through suffering—not through an easy life. The manner in which Christians deal with stress also testifies to the power of Jesus Christ. The next time you feel overwhelmed by life's problems, look for ways that God is bringing good out of the stress you face.

15. *In what specific ways do you need to change your attitude toward the stress in your life?*

16. What spiritual lesson can you learn from a difficulty you are currently facing?

◆◆◆◆ **SUPPLEMENTAL QUESTIONS**

Read Genesis 50:15-21.

> God brought good out of all of Joseph's misfortunes. The stressful experiences in his life taught him that God brings good from evil for those who trust him. You can trust him because, as Joseph learned, God can override people's evil intentions to bring about his intended results.

17. What misfortunes has God used for good in your life?

18. What is a current difficult circumstance in your life? How do you suppose God could use it for good?

19. How can you show that you trust God to work all things together for good?

Read 2 Corinthians 1:3-5.

> Many people think that when God comforts them, their troubles should go away. But if that were always so, people would turn to God only out of a desire to be relieved of pain and not out of love for him. Christians must understand that being comforted can also mean receiving strength, encouragement, and hope to deal with their troubles. The more they suffer, the more comfort God gives them. If you are feeling overwhelmed by the stress and pain in your life,

allow God to comfort you. Remember that every trial you endure will help you comfort other people who are going through similar experiences.

20. How has someone comforted you when you were stressed out or suffering?

21. What lessons have you learned from present difficulties?

22. Whom can you encourage with these lessons?

Read 2 Corinthians 4:16-18.

Christians' troubles should not diminish their faith or disillusion them. They should realize that there is a purpose for their suffering. Stress and problems have several benefits: (1) They remind us of Christ's suffering for us; (2) they keep us from pride; (3) they prove our faith to others; and (4) they give God the opportunity to demonstrate his power.

23. How does focusing our attention on Christ help us to get through our suffering?

Read James 1:2-3.

James does not say if you face trials, but whenever you face them. He assumes that Christians will have trials and that it is possible to profit from them. The point is not to pretend to be happy when facing pain, but to have a positive outlook. In other words, do two things to handle stress in your life: Expect it, and try to learn from it.

24. *What will be the demands of family, work, school, church, and other activities this week?*

25. *What is your usual reaction to these stresses?*

26. *How would responding joyfully make a difference in your life?*

27. *What can you do to prepare yourself to respond joyfully?*

LESSON TWO

Stressed to Kill

••

If you suffer from headaches, back-aches, allergies, or high blood pressure, stress could be a significant contributing factor. In fact, experts agree that most diseases are stress and lifestyle related. Beyond the physical effects, however, stress takes its toll on spiritual health. Christians must recognize the dangers of stress so they can take action before they succumb to its pressures. This lesson will help you to iden-tify the negative effects of stress on your spir-itual life and to know when to reduce the level of stress in your life.

♦♦♦♦ *STARTER*

1. *What negative side effects have you experienced from stress?*

2. *How do you know when you are under too much stress?*

◆◆◆◆◆◆◆ *STUDY*

Read the following three sets of Bible passages and application notes. Answer the questions for each set before moving on to the next.

Mark 14:33-34, 38

KJV	NIV	NLT
And he taketh with him Peter and James and John, and began to be sore amazed, and to be very heavy; and saith unto them, My soul is exceeding sorrowful unto death: tarry ye here, and watch. . . . Watch ye and pray, lest ye enter into temptation. The spirit truly is ready, but the flesh is weak.	He took Peter, James and John along with him, and he began to be deeply distressed and troubled. "My soul is overwhelmed with sorrow to the point of death," he said to them. "Stay here and keep watch. . . . Watch and pray so that you will not fall into temptation. The spirit is willing, but the body is weak."	He took Peter, James, and John with him, and he began to be filled with horror and deep distress. He told them, "My soul is crushed with grief to the point of death. Stay here and watch with me. . . . Keep alert and pray. Otherwise, temptation will overpower you. For though the spirit is willing enough, the body is weak."

In times of great stress, a person is vulnerable to temptation, even if he or she wants to resist. Jesus' disciples wanted to support him during this time of sorrow and pain, but they succumbed to temptation and missed the opportunity to help him in his hour of need. If you are under so much stress that you feel helpless to resist temptation, you may need to look for a way to eliminate or reduce some of the pressures in your life.

3. *How do you usually respond when you feel distressed or troubled?*

4. *What are some steps Christians can take to prevent themselves from falling into temptation when they are under a lot of stress?*

5.   *How can Christian friends help each other through difficult times?*

6.   *If you feel vulnerable to temptation, how could you eliminate or reduce some of the pressures in your life?*

Luke 23:20, 23-25

KJV	NIV	NLT
Pilate therefore, willing to release Jesus, spake again to them. . . . And they were instant with loud voices, requiring that he might be crucified. And the voices of them and of the chief priests prevailed. And Pilate gave sentence that it should be as they required. And he released unto them him that for sedition and murder was cast into prison, whom they had desired; but he delivered Jesus to their will.	Wanting to release Jesus, Pilate appealed to them [the chief priests, the rulers, and the people] again. . . . But with loud shouts they insistently demanded that he be crucified, and their shouts prevailed. So Pilate decided to grant their demand. He released the man who had been thrown into prison for insurrection and murder, the one they asked for, and surrendered Jesus to their will.	Pilate argued with them, because he wanted to release Jesus. . . . But the crowd shouted louder and louder for Jesus' death, and their voices prevailed. So Pilate sentenced Jesus to die as they demanded. As they had requested, he released Barabbas, the man in prison for insurrection and murder. But he delivered Jesus over to them to do as they wished.

When the stakes are high and the pressure is on, it is difficult to stand up for what is right. Had Pilate been a man of real courage, he would have released Jesus no matter what the consequences. But the crowd roared, and Pilate buckled. Holding on to moral standards under social or political pressure can produce a high level of stress in us. Taking the easy way out, as Pilate did, may relieve the stress but leave us with a burden of guilt to deal with later.

7. Why are most people so vulnerable to peer pressure?

8. What has helped you stand up for your faith despite negative pressure from others?

9. In what area of your life are you most in danger of compromising your beliefs or moral standards because of stress?

10. How can you better equip yourself to stand strong under this pressure?

Mark 4:14-17

KJV	NIV	NLT
The sower soweth the word. And these are they by the way side, where the word is sown; but when they have heard, Satan cometh immediately, and taketh away the word that was sown in their hearts. And these are they likewise which are sown on stony ground; who, when they have heard the word, immediately receive it with gladness; and have no root in themselves, and so endure but for a time: afterward, when affliction or persecution ariseth for the word's sake, immediately they are offended.	The farmer sows the word. Some people are like seed along the path, where the word is sown. As soon as they hear it, Satan comes and takes away the word that was sown in them. Others, like seed sown on rocky places, hear the word and at once receive it with joy. But since they have no root, they last only a short time. When trouble or persecution comes because of the word, they quickly fall away.	The farmer I talked about is the one who brings God's message to others. The seed that fell on the hard path represents those who hear the message, but then Satan comes at once and takes it away from them. The rocky soil represents those who hear the message and receive it with joy. But like young plants in such soil, their roots don't go very deep. At first they get along fine, but they wilt as soon as they have problems or are persecuted because they believe the word.

In this parable, Jesus said that the pressures of life cause some people to abandon their faith in God. They fall away because they do not have roots. Some Christians experience such tremendous stress that they get distracted from their desire to obey Christ. Do not allow the problems in your life to overwhelm you. Let your problems push you toward Christ, rather than away. Then the roots of your faith will grow stronger and deeper.

11. *What trials or difficulties cause some believers to fall away?*

12. *When have you felt overwhelmed by your problems?*

13. *What pressures do you face now that could weaken your Christian commitment?*

14. *How can you make sure that stress does not choke out the life of your Christian walk?*

◆◆◆◆◆◆ **SUMMARY**

You have learned from these three passages that stress can make Christians vulnerable to temptation, weaken their resolve to stand against peer pressure, and even push them to compromise their faith. To protect yourself, you must acknowledge the power of stress and be willing to take steps to reduce it when it threatens your spiritual health.

15. *What steps can you take this week to reduce or better manage the stress in your life?*

◆◆◆◆◆◆ **SUPPLEMENTAL QUESTIONS**

Read Matthew 14:6-10.

Herod did not want to kill John the Baptist, but he gave the order so that he would not be embarrassed in front of his guests. How easy it is to give in to the crowd and to be pressured into doing wrong! Peer pressure often tempts Christians to compromise their faith. Determine to do what is right, no matter how much pressure you face.

16. *When are you likely to promise more than you will want to pay?*

17. *In what circumstances do you feel the most pressure to please the crowd?*

Read Proverbs 4:14-17; 10:12; 12:16-21.

> *Relationships that cause us to fall bring only additional stress to everyday life. But this stress is unnecessary and even avoidable. By choosing our friends carefully, we can eliminate the stress caused by hanging around with the wrong crowd. And God has provided us with the wisdom we need to choose friends carefully and limit the stress in our lives. This wisdom is found in Proverbs. If you heed it, you will not add to—and you may even decrease—the amount of stress already in your life.*

18. *Which friendships are the most stressful for you to maintain?*

19. *How can you keep the friendship but reduce the stress?*

20. *How can you bring more peace than stress to your friendships?*

Read Hebrews 10:23-25.

> *Stress can cause people to reshuffle priorities. The pressure of a deadline can loom over every other activity. The temptation can be to skip church, ignore friends, or neglect family. Make sure you stay involved with other believers when the pressure is on.*

21. *What is a way you can encourage someone to remain faithful to God, family, and friends even through their difficult times?*

22. *What is the most encouraging thing someone can do for you when you are under a great deal of stress?*

LESSON THREE

Worth the Hassle

••

Many people want to avoid pain and problems at all cost. But Scripture clearly teaches that there is one kind of stress Christians should not try to avoid. When they experience problems and persecution because of their allegiance to Christ, they should accept these trials as part of the cost of following him. This lesson will teach you how to handle the trials that come as a result of your faith in Christ.

◆◆◆◆ STARTER

1. *What tricks or techniques do children use to escape the consequences of their misbehavior?*

2. *What is something for which you were wrongly punished when you were growing up?*

◆◆◆◆◆◆ **STUDY**

Read the following three sets of Bible passages and application notes.
Answer the questions for each set before moving on to the next.

Matthew 10:34-36

KJV	NIV	NLT
Think not that I am come to send peace on earth: I came not to send peace, but a sword. For I am come to set a man at variance against his father, and the daughter against her mother, and the daughter in law against her mother in law. And a man's foes shall be they of his own household.	Do not suppose that I have come to bring peace to the earth. I did not come to bring peace, but a sword. For I have come to turn "a man against his father, a daughter against her mother, a daughter-in-law against her mother-in-law—a man's enemies will be the members of his own household."	Don't imagine that I came to bring peace to the earth! No, I came to bring a sword. I have come to set a man against his father, and a daughter against her mother, and a daughter-in-law against her mother-in-law. Your enemies will be right in your own household!

Jesus does not bring the kind of peace that glosses over deep differences just for the sake of superficial harmony. Conflict and disagreement will arise between those who choose to follow Christ and those who do not. In saying this, Jesus was not encouraging Christians to stir up dissension. Rather, he was showing that his presence demands a decision. Because some will follow him and some will not, conflict will inevitably arise. As you follow Christ, expect to face problems and significant personal stress because of your faith in him.

3. *What is your natural response to problems and pain?*

4. *When has your faith created family problems?*

5. *How does this passage of Scripture change your attitude toward stress?*

6. *What do you want to remember the next time you encounter conflict because of your faith in Christ?*

---

1 Thessalonians 3:2-4

KJV	NIV	NLT
[We] sent Timotheus, our brother, and minister of God, and our fellow-labourer in the gospel of Christ, to establish you, and to comfort you concerning your faith: That no man should be moved by these afflictions: for yourselves know that we are appointed thereunto. For verily, when we were with you, we told you before that we should suffer tribulation; even as it came to pass, and ye know.	We sent Timothy, who is our brother and God's fellow worker in spreading the gospel of Christ, to strengthen and encourage you in your faith, so that no one would be unsettled by these trials. You know quite well that we were destined for them. In fact, when we were with you, we kept telling you that we would be persecuted. And it turned out that way, as you well know.	We sent Timothy to visit you. He is our co-worker for God and our brother in proclaiming the Good News of Christ. We sent him to strengthen you, to encourage you in your faith, and to keep you from becoming disturbed by the troubles you were going through. But, of course, you know that such troubles are going to happen to us Christians. Even while we were with you, we warned you that troubles would soon come—and they did, as you well know.

Obeying God in a fallen world sometimes brings its own kind of pressure and problems. It's difficult for many believers to accept the fact that difficulties in life may result from doing what is right. When they stand up for the truth or proclaim the gospel, some people will choose to reject both the message and the messenger. Rather than looking for a way out, accept the trials, and ask God to give you the strength to handle the stressful situations well.

7. When have you endured pressure or rejection because of your faith?

8. How would you answer a Christian who wonders why God allows his people to suffer?

9. If we assume troubles will come, what aspects of the Christian life will become more meaningful to us?

10. From what Christian friend can you draw encouragement and strength in standing up for your faith under stress?

---

1 Peter 4:12, 14, 16

KJV	NIV	NLT
Beloved, think it not strange concerning the fiery trial which is to try you, as though some strange thing happened unto you. . . . If ye be reproached for the name of Christ, happy are ye; for the spirit of glory and of God resteth upon you: on their part he is evil spoken of, but on your part he is glorified. . . . Yet if any man suffer as a Christian, let him not be ashamed; but let him glorify God on this behalf.	Dear friends, do not be surprised at the painful trial you are suffering, as though something strange were happening to you. . . . If you are insulted because of the name of Christ, you are blessed, for the Spirit of glory and of God rests on you. . . . However, if you suffer as a Christian, do not be ashamed, but praise God that you bear that name.	Dear friends, don't be surprised at the fiery trials you are going through, as if something strange were happening to you. . . . Be happy if you are insulted for being a Christian, for then the glorious Spirit of God will come upon you. . . . But it is no shame to suffer for being a Christian. Praise God for the privilege of being called by his wonderful name!

Peter reminds Christians that suffering for their faith is unavoidable. But they can choose their response: They can find an excuse to give in to the pressure, or they can trust God through it all. When you suffer because of your loyalty to Christ, remember that God has sent his Spirit to be with you. Depend on him to help you joyfully accept and endure the pressure.

11. *Under what circumstances is it tempting to hide one's faith or be ashamed of it?*

12. *Why do you think some Christians have never had to suffer for their faith?*

13. *What price have you had to pay to stand up for your beliefs?*

14. *How can you learn to rejoice even when facing persecution or difficult pressure?*

◆◆◆◆◆◆ **SUMMARY**

These three passages warn us to expect trials and problems in life because of our faith in God. Instead of trying to avoid these conflicts, we should accept them and consider it a privilege to suffer for the sake of Christ. The next time you face stress because of your faith, resist the temptation to fold under the pressure. Stand strong in God's power. In light of eternity, suffering for Christ's sake is worth every minute!

15. *What are you willing to risk to stand up for your faith in Christ?*

16. *How do you want to respond the next time you have to endure stress or conflict for the sake of Christ?*

◆◆◆◆ SUPPLEMENTAL QUESTIONS

Read Acts 5:27-42.

> *The apostles knew their priorities. While we should try to live at peace with everyone, conflict with the world and its authorities is sometimes inevitable for a Christian. There will be situations where you cannot obey both God and man. Then you must obey God and trust his Word.*

17. Who was the ultimate authority in the apostles' lives?

18. When you are forced to choose between obeying God or people, what makes it easier to obey God rather than people?

19. What are you willing to sacrifice in exchange for sharing the gospel—your life, your friends, your job?

Read John 15:18.

> *Christians will get plenty of hatred from the world. Sometimes this hatred will come from authorities who are angry at those Christians who refuse to do wrong. Such authorities may punish Christians for obeying God rather than them. Despite the stress the authorities may cause in our lives, we should not be swayed to compromise our obedience to God. Let Jesus' words in Luke 6:22 encourage you to be obedient to him under the threat of punishment: "Blessed are you when men hate you, when they exclude you and insult you and reject your name as evil, because of the Son of Man" (NIV).*

20. When have you had to disobey someone in authority in order to be obedient to God?

21. *What were the consequences of your choice?*

22. *Is it easier or harder to obey God instead of human authorities when you are unsure of the consequences you will face? Explain.*

Read Luke 12:51-53.

> *In these strange and unsettling words, Jesus revealed that his coming would result in conflict. That is because there is no middle ground with Jesus. Loyalties must be declared and commitments made, sometimes to the point of severing other relationships. Are you willing to risk your family's disapproval in order to serve Christ?*

23. *Why is following Christ worth risking even family relationships?*

24. *How can you encourage another Christian who has been disowned by family or friends?*

LESSON FOUR

Face the Facts

••

Not all suffering is the result of good Christian conduct. Sometimes a person may grumble, "He's just picking on me because I'm a Christian." However, it may be that it is the person's own unpleasant behavior that is the cause of the problem. It often takes careful thought or wise counsel to determine the real cause of suffering. This lesson will help you recognize when your own mistakes are the cause of your stress. It will also teach you how to guard against self-inflicted stress.

◆◆◆◆ STARTER

1. *What do you think are the most common causes of stress?*

2. *When have you ever felt like you were getting more than your fair share of problems and pressures?*

◆◆◆◆◆◆ **STUDY**

Read the following three sets of Bible passages and application notes. Answer the questions for each set before moving on to the next.

Genesis 20:1-2

KJV	NIV	NLT
And Abraham journeyed from thence toward the south country, and dwelled between Kadesh and Shur, and sojourned in Gerar. And Abraham said of Sarah his wife, She is my sister: and Abimelech king of Gerar sent, and took Sarah.	Now Abraham moved on from there into the region of the Negev and lived between Kadesh and Shur. For a while he stayed in Gerar, and there Abraham said of his wife Sarah, "She is my sister." Then Abimelech king of Gerar sent for Sarah and took her.	Now Abraham moved south to the Negev and settled for a while between Kadesh and Shur at a place called Gerar. Abraham told people there that his wife, Sarah, was his sister. So King Abimelech sent for her and had her brought to him at his palace.

When Abimelech took Sarah to be his wife, God revealed to him in a dream that he was in danger of committing adultery because she was already married. Abimelech confronted Abraham, demanding to know why Abraham had brought guilt on the kingdom. Abraham had to admit his sin and ask the Lord to reverse his punishment on Abimelech's household. Abraham caused a whole kingdom to suffer and put himself and his wife in great danger because of his lack of trust in God. Fortunately for Abraham, Abimelech treated him kindly, returning Sarah along with gifts of cattle and slaves. Disobedience to God can also bring tremendous stress today. People need to recognize when their problems are the result of their own mistakes and quickly confess their sin to the Lord.

3. *How can a Christian know when stress is caused by his or her own sin?*

4. *Why do believers often choose to do what is wrong, even when they know the risks and potential consequences?*

5. *Why do you think God sometimes protects people from the consequences of their mistakes?*

6. *What steps do you need to take this week to reduce your risk of suffering unnecessarily?*

Exodus 16:2-3

KJV	NIV	NLT
And the whole congregation of the children of Israel murmured against Moses and Aaron in the wilderness: And the children of Israel said unto them, Would to God we had died by the hand of the LORD in the land of Egypt, when we sat by the flesh pots, and when we did eat bread to the full; for ye have brought us forth into this wilderness, to kill this whole assembly with hunger.	In the desert the whole community grumbled against Moses and Aaron. The Israelites said to them, "If only we had died by the LORD's hand in Egypt! There we sat around pots of meat and ate all the food we wanted, but you have brought us out into this desert to starve this entire assembly to death."	There, too, the whole community of Israel spoke bitterly against Moses and Aaron. "Oh, that we were back in Egypt," they moaned. "It would have been better if the LORD had killed us there! At least there we had plenty to eat. But now you have brought us into this desert to starve us to death.

The Israelites should have known from past experience that God would provide for their needs. Instead, they complained bitterly about the dangers, shortages, and inconveniences of desert life and longed to be back in Egypt. In the pressure of the moment, they did not trust God. Instead, they wished for the quickest way of escape. Refusing to trust God when we face difficult circumstances usually makes matters even worse for us and increases our stress.

7. What problems or pressures can result from a person's lack of trust in God?

8. Why is it especially difficult to trust in God when we are under pressure?

9. How do you respond to stress caused by your own sin?

10. What would help you to trust God more when you are under pressure?

James 4:1-2

KJV	NIV	NLT
From whence come wars and fightings among you? come they not hence, even of your lusts that war in your members? Ye lust, and have not: ye kill, and desire to have, and cannot obtain: ye fight and war, yet ye have not, because ye ask not.	What causes fights and quarrels among you? Don't they come from your desires that battle within you? You want something but don't get it. You kill and covet, but you cannot have what you want. You quarrel and fight. You do not have because you do not ask God.	What is causing the quarrels and fights among you? Isn't it the whole army of evil desires at war within you? You want what you don't have, so you scheme and kill to get it. You are jealous for what others have, and can't possess it, so you fight and quarrel to take it away from them. And yet the reason you don't have what you want is that you don't ask God for it.

Conflict with others causes much of the stress that people experience. James explains that quarrels and disputes result from evil desires battling within. People want more possessions, more money, higher status, and more recognition. So they fight with others to fulfill these desires. When you cannot seem to get along with anyone, ask yourself if unrealistic expectations or selfish desires could be causing some of these problems. If so, you need to deal with your sin before you can begin to resolve the conflicts and reduce your level of stress.

11. *What are some typical causes of conflict between friends and family members?*

12. *When have your unrealistic expectations or selfish desires caused tension in your relationships with others?*

13. *How do you know when it is right or wrong to fight?*

14. *Where can you turn to find help to deal with unhealthy expectations and desires?*

♦♦♦♦♦♦♦ **SUMMARY**

These three passages reveal that stress is often needlessly caused by a person's own actions. When someone chooses to disobey God, refuses to trust in him, or succumbs to his or her own evil desires, it usually results in unnecessary stress. When pressure comes your way, ask God to help you identify the cause of your stress. If it is the result of your own sin, take responsibility for your actions. Face the facts and make things right!

15. *For what pressures in your life can you take responsibility?*

16. *What can you do to reduce or eliminate these pressures?*

◆◆◆◆◆ SUPPLEMENTAL QUESTIONS

Read John 5:44; Galatians 1:10; and 1 Thessalonians 2:4.

> *It is only natural for people to want to make their friends, family, and bosses happy. But much of the stress people suffer comes when they focus their efforts on pleasing others instead of God.*

17. *What have you done recently to please or impress others?*

18. *What have you done today to please the Lord?*

Read Colossians 3:23-24.

> *Since the Creation, God has given people work to do. Regarding our work as an act of worship or service to God would reduce some of the stress and pressure we experience on the job. Christians could work without complaining or resentment if they would treat their job-related problems as the cost of discipleship. The right perspective could also protect them from over-committing themselves simply to impress others.*

19. *What should be a believer's ultimate goal on the job?*

20. *To what degree do you exhibit this goal in your life?*

Read Galatians 6:4-5.

> *Comparing yourself with others causes unnecessary stress. People make comparisons for many reasons. Some point out others' faults in order to feel better about themselves. Others simply want reassurance that they are doing well. When you are tempted to compare yourself with*

others, look to Jesus Christ. His example will inspire you to do your very best, without worrying about what others have done.

21. Who are you likely to compare yourself with on the job? at home? in the church?

22. What are your motivations for comparing yourself with others?

23. Why is it better to compare yourself with Christ rather than with other people?

LESSON FIVE

Outer Stress, Inner Peace

••

Like it or not, we face some level of stress in every area of life. Thankfully, stress on the outside need not mean stress on the inside. Contrary to popular belief, true peace is not found in positive thinking, in absence of conflict, or in good feelings. It comes from knowing that God is in control and trusting him with all of your heart. This lesson will motivate you to turn to God for help during your trials, instead of relying only on your own strength to get you through.

◆◆◆◆ *STARTER*

1. *What is some of the popular advice today for dealing with stress?*

2. *What advice, if any, have you found most effective for reducing stress?*

◆◆◆◆◆◆◆ **STUDY**

Read the following three sets of Bible passages and application notes. Answer the questions for each set before moving on to the next.

Psalm 3:1, 3-6

KJV	NIV	NLT
LORD, how are they increased that trouble me! many are they that rise up against me. . . . But thou, O LORD, art a shield for me; my glory, and the lifter up of mine head. I cried unto the LORD with my voice, and he heard me out of his holy hill. Selah. I laid me down and slept; I awaked; for the LORD sustained me. I will not be afraid of ten thousands of people, that have set themselves against me round about.	O LORD, how many are my foes! How many rise up against me! . . . But you are a shield around me, O LORD; you bestow glory on me and lift up my head. To the LORD I cry aloud, and he answers me from his holy hill. I lie down and sleep; I wake again, because the LORD sustains me. I will not fear the tens of thousands drawn up against me on every side.	O LORD, I have so many enemies; so many are against me. . . . But you, O LORD, are a shield around me, my glory, and the one who lifts my head high. I cried out to the LORD, and he answered me from his holy mountain. *Interlude* I lay down and slept. I woke up in safety, for the LORD was watching over me. I am not afraid of ten thousand enemies who surround me on every side.

Sleep does not come easily during a crisis. David could have had sleepless nights when his son Absalom rebelled and gathered an army to kill him. But he slept peacefully, even during the stress of a rebellion. What made the difference? David cried out to the Lord, and the Lord heard him. The assurance of answered prayer brings peace. If you are lying awake at night worrying about matters that you cannot control, pour out your heart to God, and thank him that he is able to control what you cannot.

3. *What often prevents Christians from turning to God in prayer during stressful times?*

4. *Some people blame God for their hardships. What happens when they do this?*

5. *How has knowing Jesus Christ helped you handle the stress in your life?*

6. *How can you rely more on God instead of yourself during difficult times?*

John 14:25-27

KJV	NIV	NLT
These things have I spoken unto you, being yet present with you. But the Comforter, which is the Holy Ghost, whom the Father will send in my name, he shall teach you all things, and bring all things to your remembrance, whatsoever I have said unto you. Peace I leave with you, my peace I give unto you: not as the world giveth, give I unto you. Let not your heart be troubled, neither let it be afraid.	All this I have spoken while still with you. But the Counselor, the Holy Spirit, whom the Father will send in my name, will teach you all things and will remind you of everything I have said to you. Peace I leave with you; my peace I give you. I do not give to you as the world gives. Do not let your hearts be troubled and do not be afraid.	I am telling you these things now while I am still with you. But when the Father sends the Counselor as my representative—and by the Counselor I mean the Holy Spirit—he will teach you everything and will remind you of everything I myself have told you. I am leaving you with a gift—peace of mind and heart! And the peace I give isn't like the peace the world gives. So don't be troubled or afraid.

The end result of the Holy Spirit's work in a person's life is deep and lasting peace. Unlike worldly peace, which is usually defined as the absence of conflict, this peace is confident assurance in any circumstance. With Christ's peace, the Christian has no need to fear the present or the future. If your life is filled with stress, ask the Holy Spirit to fill you with his peace.

7. When have you been comforted by the Holy Spirit?

8. What were the circumstances surrounding your experience of his comfort?

9. How did this peace differ from that of the world?

10. In what area of your life would you like to experience more of God's peace?

Philippians 4:4, 6-7

KJV	NIV	NLT
Rejoice in the Lord alway: and again I say, Rejoice. . . . Be careful for nothing; but in every thing by prayer and supplication with thanksgiving let your requests be made known unto God. And the peace of God, which passeth all understanding, shall keep your hearts and minds through Christ Jesus.	Rejoice in the Lord always. I will say it again: Rejoice! . . . Do not be anxious about anything, but in everything, by prayer and petition, with thanksgiving, present your requests to God. And the peace of God, which transcends all understanding, will guard your hearts and your minds in Christ Jesus.	Always be full of joy in the Lord. I say it again—rejoice! . . . Don't worry about anything; instead, pray about everything. Tell God what you need and thank him for all he has done. If you do this, you will experience God's peace, which is far more wonderful than the human mind can understand. His peace will guard your hearts and minds as you live in Christ Jesus.

It seems strange that a man in prison would be telling a church to rejoice. But Paul's attitude teaches an important lesson: Circumstances do not have to affect one's inner peace. Paul was full of joy because he knew that no matter what happened to him, Jesus was with him. As Christians, we can easily get discouraged about the pain and stress we have to endure. But remember that God wants you to depend on him during those difficult times instead of relying on yourself or others to get you through.

11. *How is it possible to have joy in the middle of a difficult situation?*

12. *How can prayer reduce stress?*

13. *What keeps you from experiencing God's peace during difficult circumstances?*

14. *How can you overcome these barriers to experiencing God's peace?*

◆◆◆◆◆◆ **SUMMARY**

How can a person find peace in the midst of stress? These three passages reveal that God is the only source of true peace. Instead of buckling under the pressures of life, Christians can turn to God in prayer and depend on the Holy Spirit to help. Let God's peace guard your heart against anxiety and stress. Then you will be able to relax in life's most difficult moments, knowing that God is in control and that he will take care of you.

15. *During times of stress, what will help you turn toward God instead of away from him?*

16. *How can you increase your dependence on God during times of stress?*

◆◆◆◆ *SUPPLEMENTAL QUESTIONS*

Read Psalm 62.

> *David expressed his feelings to God and then reaffirmed his faith. Prayer can release tensions in times of emotional stress. Trusting God to be your rock, salvation, and fortress will change your entire outlook on life. When you are resting in God's strength, even the greatest stress cannot shake you.*

17. What is your first reaction to stress?

18. What role has prayer played in dealing with your stress?

19. How can you learn to rely on God's strength rather than your own?

Read Psalms 18:16; 31:9; 55:17; 69:29; and 102:2.

> *Many Christians turn to the psalms during stressful times. In them, they take comfort from the fact that God cares for and protects those he loves. When you are stressed, read through some of the psalms, and let God comfort you through his Word.*

20. How do the psalmists respond to stressful times?

21. What can you learn from their responses?

Read John 15:9-11.

> *When things are going well, people feel elated. When hardships come, they may sink into depression. But true joy transcends the rolling waves of circumstances. Joy comes from a consistent relationship with Jesus Christ. When your life is intertwined with his, he will help you walk through adversity without sinking into debilitating lows. The joy of living with Jesus Christ daily will keep you levelheaded, no matter what your situation.*

22. *Which commands of Jesus are the hardest for you to keep?*

23. *What could possibly be joyful about keeping these commands?*

24. *What steps can you take this week to start obeying these commands?*

Read Romans 8:28.

> *God constantly works in the circumstances of Christians. We can have confidence that he orchestrates events as he desires.*

25. *Can anything thwart God's plans?*

26. *What should be your response to stressful circumstances that are beyond your control?*

LESSON SIX

Tense Relationships

• •

Scripture is filled with stories of people who faced conflict with others. In fact, some of the great heroes of the Bible suffered from broken or strained relationships. In the same way, much of the stress that Christians experience comes from disagreements with friends or relatives. By examining biblical examples, this lesson will help you reduce conflict in your relationships and thereby decrease unnecessary stress.

◆◆◆◆ STARTER

1. *To what degree do relationships raise your stress level?*

2. *What are some of the typical approaches people use to resolve conflict or disagreements?*

◆◆◆◆◆◆ **STUDY**

Read the following three sets of Bible passages and application notes.
Answer the questions for each set before moving on to the next.

Genesis 13:5-9

KJV	NIV	NLT
And Lot also, which went with Abram, had flocks, and herds, and tents. And the land was not able to bear them, that they might dwell together: for their substance was great, so that they could not dwell together. And there was a strife between the herdmen of Abram's cattle and the herdmen of Lot's cattle: and the Canaanite and the Perizzite dwelled then in the land. And Abram said unto Lot, Let there be no strife, I pray thee, between me and thee, and between my herdmen and thy herdmen; for we be brethren. Is not the whole land before thee? separate thyself, I pray thee, from me: if thou wilt take the left hand, then I will go to the right; or if thou depart to the right hand, then I will go to the left.	Now Lot, who was moving about with Abram, also had flocks and herds and tents. But the land could not support them while they stayed together, for their possessions were so great that they were not able to stay together. And quarreling arose between Abram's herdsmen and the herdsmen of Lot. The Canaanites and Perizzites were also living in the land at that time. So Abram said to Lot, "Let's not have any quarreling between you and me, or between your herdsmen and mine, for we are brothers. Is not the whole land before you? Let's part company. If you go to the left, I'll go to the right; if you go to the right, I'll go to the left."	Now Lot, who was traveling with Abram, was also very wealthy with sheep, cattle, and many tents. But the land could not support both Abram and Lot with all their flocks and herds living so close together. There were too many animals for the available pastureland. So an argument broke out between the herdsmen of Abram and Lot. At that time Canaanites and Perizzites were also living in the land. Then Abram talked it over with Lot. "This arguing between our herdsmen has got to stop," he said. "After all, we are close relatives! I'll tell you what we'll do. Take your choice of any section of the land you want, and we will separate. If you want that area over there, then I'll stay here. If you want to stay in this area, then I'll move on to another place.

Facing a potential conflict with his nephew Lot, Abram took the initiative in settling the dispute. He gave Lot first choice, even though Abram, being older, had the right to choose first. Abram also showed a willingness to risk being cheated. Abram's example shows how to respond to stressful family situations: (1) Take the initiative in resolving conflicts; (2) let others have first choice, even if that means not getting what you want; and (3) put family peace above personal desires. Following these guidelines will help to eliminate much of the stress from family conflicts.

3. What often prevents people from getting along with others?

4. What personal sacrifices sometimes have to be made to resolve conflict?

5. In what situations is it most difficult to take the first step toward resolving conflict with others?

6. To what relationship do you want to apply the principles from this passage?

Genesis 26:19-22

KJV	NIV	NLT
And Isaac's servants digged in the valley, and found there a well of springing water. And the herdmen of Gerar did strive with Isaac's herdmen, saying, The water is ours: and he called the name of the well Esek; because they strove with him. And they digged another well, and strove for that also: and he called the name of it Sitnah. And he removed from thence, and digged another well; and for that they strove not: and he called the name of it Rehoboth; and he said, For now the LORD hath made room for us, and we shall be fruitful in the land.	Isaac's servants dug in the valley and discovered a well of fresh water there. But the herdsmen of Gerar quarreled with Isaac's herdsmen and said, "The water is ours!" So he named the well Esek, because they disputed with him. Then they dug another well, but they quarreled over that one also; so he named it Sitnah. He moved on from there and dug another well, and no one quarreled over it. He named it Rehoboth, saying, "Now the LORD has given us room and we will flourish in the land."	His shepherds also dug in the Gerar Valley and found a gushing spring. But then the local shepherds came and claimed the spring. "This is our water," they said, and they argued over it with Isaac's herdsmen. So Isaac named the well "Argument," because they had argued about it with him. Isaac's men then dug another well, but again there was a fight over it. So Isaac named it "Opposition." Abandoning that one, he dug another well, and the local people finally left him alone. So Isaac called it "Room Enough," for he said, "At last the LORD has made room for us, and we will be able to thrive."

Three times Isaac and his men dug new wells. When the first two disputes arose, Isaac moved on. Finally there was enough room for everyone. Rather than start an argument, and possibly a huge fight, Isaac compromised for the sake of peace. When disputes and disagreements with others have you feeling helpless and discouraged, consider letting go of some of your wants, desires, or even rights in order to reduce the stress.

7. *When is it better to give up or give in for the sake of peace?*

8. *How can a person know when to give up his or her desires or rights in a bad situation?*

9. *What can a person do to resolve a conflict with a friend who is not interested in reconciliation?*

10. *What rights or desires are you willing to give up to make peace with a friend?*

Numbers 12:1-2

KJV	NIV	NLT
And Miriam and Aaron spake against Moses because of the Ethiopian woman whom he had married: for he had married an Ethiopian woman. And they said, Hath the LORD indeed spoken only by Moses? hath he not spoken also by us? And the LORD heard it.	Miriam and Aaron began to talk against Moses because of his Cushite wife, for he had married a Cushite. "Has the LORD spoken only through Moses?" they asked. "Hasn't he also spoken through us?" And the LORD heard this.	While they were at Hazeroth, Miriam and Aaron criticized Moses because he had married a Cushite woman. They said, "Has the LORD spoken only through Moses? Hasn't he spoken through us, too?" But the LORD heard them.

People often argue over minor matters, conveniently missing the real issue. Such was the case when Miriam and Aaron came to Moses with their complaint. Since they could not find fault with the way Moses was leading the people, they chose to criticize his wife. The real issue, however, was their growing jealousy of Moses' position and influence. Rather than face the problem squarely by dealing with their envy and pride, they chose to create a diversion. When you are involved in a disagreement, stop and ask yourself if you are arguing over the real issue or if you have created a diversion by attacking someone's character. Then ask God to help you identify the real issue and deal with it appropriately.

11. *How do jealousy and pride create conflict?*

12. *Why do people often avoid dealing with the real issues behind their broken relationships?*

13. *In what relationship have you created a diversion instead of working on the real problem?*

14. *What are you willing to do to resolve the conflict in this particular relationship?*

◆ ◆ ◆ ◆ ◆ **SUMMARY**

These three passages give practical advice on how to resolve conflict in
relationships: Take the initiative in resolving disagreements, value the relationship above your own desires, and confront the real problems instead of
arguing about secondary issues. By following these biblical principles, you
can reduce much of the stress that comes from strained or broken relationships.

15. *In light of these verses, what specific changes do you need to make
in the way you relate to your friends and family?*

16. *What biblical principle do you think will help you the most to avoid
or reduce the stress caused by strained relationships?*

◆ ◆ ◆ ◆ ◆ **SUPPLEMENTAL QUESTIONS**

Read Joshua 22:9-34.

*When the tribes of Reuben and Gad and the half-tribe of Manasseh built an altar at the Jordan
River, the rest of Israel feared that these tribes were starting their own religion and rebelling
against God. But before beginning an all-out war, Phinehas led a delegation to learn the truth. He
was willing to negotiate rather than fight if a battle was not necessary. When he learned that the
altar was for a memorial rather than for pagan sacrifice, war was averted and unity restored. Christians would benefit from a similar approach to resolving conflicts. Assuming the worst about the
intentions of others only brings trouble. Instead, stop and listen to what others have to say, and
do not react until you have heard the whole story.*

17. *Would you say that you are quicker to condemn someone or give that person the benefit of the doubt?*

18. *When you hear a divisive rumor about someone, what can you do to determine if the rumor is true?*

Read 2 Samuel 2:1–3:1.

> *The events recorded in this passage led to a long war between David's followers and the troops loyal to Ish-bosheth and Abner. This war occurred because Israel and Judah had lost sight of God's vision and purpose. Instead of uniting to accomplish the same goals, they fought each other. When you face conflict, step back from the hostilities and consider whether you and your enemy have common goals that are bigger than your differences. Appeal to those interests as you work for a settlement.*

19. *In this passage, what was the cost of unchecked conflict?*

20. *What can this kind of conflict do to a church?*

21. *How can you work to keep peace at church—even though different groups have different opinions?*

Read Matthew 18:15-17.

> *These are Jesus' guidelines for dealing with conflict. They concern (1) Christians, not unbelievers, (2) sins committed against you, not others, and (3) conflict resolution in the context of the church, not the community at large. Jesus' words are not a license for a frontal*

attack on every person who hurts or slights you. They are not a license to start a destructive gossip campaign or to call for a church trial. They are designed to reconcile those who disagree so that all Christians can live in harmony.

22. *When someone hurts you, how would you prefer to respond?*

23. *How does Jesus' teaching differ from that?*

Read 2 Corinthians 13:11.

Paul closed this letter to the Corinthians with an admonition to "live in peace" (NIV). Living in peace does not come through glossing over problems, conflicts, and difficulties. Peace is also not produced by neglect, denial, withdrawal, or bitterness. Rather, it is the by-product of hard work and problem solving. Just as Paul and the Corinthians had to hammer out difficulties to bring peace, so you should apply these principles to your relationships with others.

24. *Who destroys your efforts to be peaceful?*

25. *To what degree do you regularly ask the "God of love and peace" to help you maintain peace with that person?*

26. *What steps can you take to initiate and keep peace?*

If you enjoyed this topical study, be sure to check out the other seven studies available on:

Character
Friendship
Money
Parenting
Priorities
Work
Worship

If your group completes one or more of the studies listed above and wants to study a book of the Bible for a change of pace, consider using one of the Life Application Bible Studies listed below. These guides help you study a book of the Bible using an application-oriented format.

Genesis TLB
Joshua TLB
Judges NIV
Ruth & Esther TLB
1 Samuel NIV
Ezra & Nehemiah NIV
Proverbs NIV
Daniel NIV
Matthew NIV
Mark NIV & TLB
Luke NIV
John NIV
Acts NIV & TLB
Romans NIV
1 Corinthians NIV
2 Corinthians NIV
Galatians & Ephesians NIV
Philippians & Colossians NIV
1 & 2 Thessalonians & Philemon NIV
1 & 2 Timothy & Titus NIV
Hebrews NIV
James NIV
1 & 2 Peter & Jude NIV
1, 2, & 3 John NIV
Revelation NIV